Introduction

This collection of rhymes provides a fun way to help children develop the early oral language that underpins successful learning and life-long success. As a primary school teacher, I observed a deleterious gap between children's school entry language skills and I became increasingly motivated to examine the language needs of all children but especially those in danger of being 'left behind'. In 2005 I set out to produce materials to support children's early language development. My journey can be summed up in the words of one six-year-old I met along the way, 'I'm always in trouble because I can't read and write my sentences'. A quick chat revealed that like too many children, this six-year-old was unable to construct or read simple sentences because they did not have the oral language to do so. Little did I know, how long my journey would take.

In 2018, and having by then completed a master's degree in child psychology and educational development, I was able to give this project my full attention. My research together with my classroom observations indicated that it was imprudent to try to address this issue without a full review of historical and contemporary research*. I completed this research in May 2020. The research findings support my classroom observations. Children entering school with poorer language skills than their peers, specifically in terms of their oral vocabulary, are vulnerable to life-long underachievement in the classroom and beyond. The research also highlights the limitations of school entry remediation. Whilst accepting that some children may be born with or develop specific language needs, it is timely to find a way to start to address the known early language skills gap. Developing reading readiness before learning to read is key.

Wizzy's Words is a set of 70, illustrated, modern, fun and silly nursery rhymes incorporating the oral vocabulary that has been shown to signal future success if developed before school entry. The rhymes, despite being developed in response to the needs of children in danger of being 'left behind', have been designed to appeal to all children from birth onwards. The rhymes also provide a launch pad for language work beyond the pre-reading stage. Drawing on the universally validated work of psychologist Leslie Rescorla, the words used, derive from the recorded utterances of babies and children as they develop their oral language. It is clear that a language skills gap has been evident in England (and beyond) for several decades and that this gap continues to be an obstacle to learning for too many children. In line with the findings of key governmental departments in England, together with the views of esteemed children's authors Michael Rosen, Philip Pullman and others, Rescorla highlights the vital components for early oral language development.

In order that children can learn to:
Hear and listen, talk and sing, think and understand, behave and read and write, children need:

To be talked to and talk with adults and others

To be read to by adults and others

To hear and learn nursery rhymes with adults and others

To learn new words with adults and others

Wizzy's Words
A language development resource for
Engaging, Educating and Empowering all children

*To read the full review see: *PLUGGING THE EARLY LANGUAGE SKILLS GAP – A literature review addressing the question: Is the importance of language development from birth being overlooked? © Jacqueline E Alexander (2020)*

Guide to Using *Wizzy's Words* 

Why

The aim of using *Wizzy's Words* is for children to learn to hear words, then to say (sing) words, then to know words. By sharing these simple rhymes with children from birth onwards, children are immediately exposed to an age-appropriate, language-rich environment to support their language development. *Wizzy's Words* can be seen as a pre-school, language launch pad. This launch pad will help to enable children to enter school with an age-appropriate level of oral vocabulary. Furthermore, with this reading readiness, children will be ready to start to learn to read and follow more formal letters, sounds, reading and spelling work across the entire curriculum.

Who

Family, friends, educators… anyone who would like to promote young children's language development from birth onwards.

Using *Wizzy's Words*

Anytime! Anyplace! Anywhere! Bed time, bath time, meal times, play times… – Make it fun! Where indicated the rhymes follow a traditional rhythm. For other rhymes the 2nd & 4th and 6th & 8th lines rhyme. The earlier rhymes in the book include the vocabulary that most two-year-old children will exhibit. An over-emphasis on age-related targets has been avoided. This allows for a child to develop a love of words by dipping into the book and learning favourite rhymes first rather than following a directed order. (The Rhyme Titles pages give the rhyme numbers and their titles, making it easy to find favourite rhymes.)

- Share the rhymes with the child/children, modelling saying/singing the words clearly and when appropriate using the carefully matched pictures to support oral language learning – use changes of voice and voice volume to add interest for you and the child/children
- When ready share and say/sing the rhymes together with the child – let them tell you about the pictures and practise using different voices and voice volumes and using different household props to act out some of the rhymes
- When ready, progress to the child saying/singing the rhymes to you – encourage lots of discussion and description using the pictures and again promote the use of different voices and props
- Use Wizzy's words in everyday activities to consolidate the child's/children's developing oral vocabulary

The aim is to build strong oral language skills and develop the child's oral vocabulary, it is not to teach the child to read the rhymes.

Next Steps

Wizzy's Words is not a contest, it is a simple-to-use method, to promote children's reading readiness before starting school. The original aim was to support children for whom poor school entry oral vocabulary hindered their educational progress. However, the book will appeal to and be a good language development resource for all children.

Wizzy's words set for each rhyme, provides a guide to the focus vocabulary being presented. Where appropriate, plurals made by adding (s) and verbs taking an (s) are given. For reference a full list of Wizzy's words is provided at the back of the book. The list is provided so that it is possible to confirm if a child is picking up Wizzy's words. Both the sets of words and the full list of Wizzy's words should be used as a guide to the oral vocabulary that a child is using/familiar with rather than as a formal assessment tool.

Wizzy's Words promotes early oral language skills. After exposure to *Wizzy's Words* most children will be ready to explore simple oral word work further and before school entry. Be guided by your child's progress, possible ideas for next steps are given below:

1. Add Wizzy's words to sentence starters to say simple 3- and 4-word sentences – e.g. – I see a…/I see the…/This is my…/I saw a…/Look at my…/Here is the…/Here is a…/I like the…/I am a…/It is a…/I like my…/Here comes the…
2. Add describing words, such as different colours or sizes, to develop more creative spoken sentences

A rush to read can leave children without the necessary oral language skills to fully access the curriculum. A child that loves hearing and saying new words will love reading words. Your child's use of oral language is the best guide for moving on to next steps in learning to read.

Rhyme Titles

Wizzy's Words

Teddy, Teddy, Little Bear

Teddy, Teddy, little bear,
You are jumping on my chair!
Far above me out of touch,
I don’t like this very much,
Teddy, Teddy, little bear,
Please stop jumping on my chair.

(1—Tune—Twinkle, Twinkle, Little Star)

Wizzy’s words

teddy little bear you jump on

my chair me out this please stop

Look! Look! Bedtime

Look, look, bedtime, shall we count sheep?
Yes you, yes you, off to sleep!
Hug for the baby, hug for the ted,
And hug for the teddy bear who's under the bed.

(2-Tune-Baa, Baa...)

Wizzy's words

look bed sheep yes you off sleep

hug baby teddy bear under

Wizzy, Wizzy...

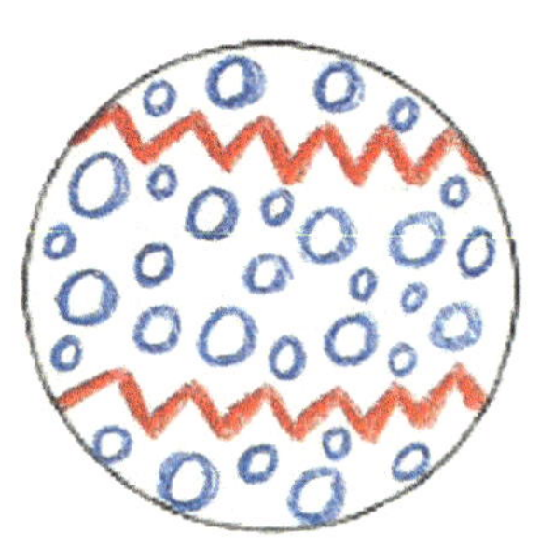

Wizzy, Wizzy, show me that ball,
Wizzy, Wizzy, show me it all.
See the red zig-zags, and see the blue rings.
Looking like flapping butterfly wings.

(3-Tune-Humpty Dumpty)

Wizzy's words

show me that ball

all see red blue look

Monday's Bowl...

Monday's bowl is full of cheese,
Tuesday's bowl is full of peas,
Wednesday's bowl is full of eggs,
Thursday's bowl is full of pegs,
Friday's bowl is heavy and cracking,
Saturday's bowl sounds like it is crashing,
So, the bowl that is full on the weekend days,
Will explode so fast and fall this way.

(4-Tune-Monday's Child...)

Wizzy's words

bowl cheese egg(s) heavy

that on this

One, Two, Hello to You

One, two, hello to you.
Three, four, who's at my door?
Five, six, have a wish.
Seven, eight, bye-bye cake!
Nine, ten, let's start again.

(5-Tune-One, Two, Buckle My Shoe)

Wizzy's words

one two hello you three four my door five six have seven eight bye-bye cake nine ten

One Two, Hello to You

One, two, hello to you.
Three, four, who's at my door?
Five, six, have a wish.
Seven, eight, bye-bye cake!
Nine, ten, let's start again.

Eleven, twelve, I hear bells.
Thirteen, fourteen, pigs are snorting.
Fifteen, sixteen, table needs fixing.
Seventeen, eighteen, bed needs making.
Nineteen, twenty, you sleep a-plenty.

(6-Tune-One, Two, Buckle My Shoe)

Wizzy's words

one two hello you three four my door

five six have seven eight bye-bye cake

nine ten pig(s) table fix bed make sleep

Rain, Rain, Go Away

Rain, rain, go away,
Come Wizzy, let's go and play.
Drippy, Wizzy wants to stay.
So, rain, splash on the path,
Getting wet just makes us laugh!

(7-Tune-Rain, Rain, Go Away)

Wizzy's words

rain go away come

want(s) on wet make(s)

Train, Train, Chuff Away

Train, train, chuff away,
Ringing your bell every day.
Ringing, ringing all the way.
Train, train, don't be shy,
Ringing as you wave bye-bye!

(8-Tune-Rain, Rain, Go Away)

Wizzy's words

train away all you bye-bye

Two Little Dinosaurs

Two little dinosaurs, playing in this room,
One being noisy, one saying zoom.
Stop making noises! Stop saying zoom!
Stop it dinos, no more booms!

(9-Tune-Two Little Dicky Birds)

Wizzy's words

two little in this room

one stop make no more

Dog and Cat...

Dog and cat sit on the mat to eat a box of biscuits,
Dog eats one, then sucks his thumb,
Then cat shows dog a pizza.
Up sits dog, and leaves the mat,
Because he is still hungry,
Dog gets a knife and cuts a slice,
Then eats pizza, oh so smugly!

(10-Tune-Jack and Jill...)

Wizzy's words

dog cat sit(s) on eat(s) biscuit(s) one

thumb show(s) pizza up

hungry knife cut(s)

The Great, Big, Bad, Old Fox

The great, big, bad, old fox had eaten seven hens,
Duck pushed them out into the chicken pen,
But they ran away again.
When they were in, they were in,
And when they were out, they were out,
But when they were only half way in,
They were neither in nor out.

(11-Tune-The Grand Old Duke of York)

Wizzy's words

big bad eat seven hen(s) duck push

out chicken ran away in out

Hungry, Hungry Chicken

Hungry, hungry chicken, my friend Ron,
Runs up the slide with his pants on.
One foot off and one foot on,
Hungry, hungry chicken, my friend Ron.

(12-Tune-Diddle, Diddle, Dumpling...)

Wizzy's words

hungry chicken my run(s) slide

pants on one foot off

Oh! Puddle, Puddle!

Oh! Puddle, puddle, let's splash in the middle,
And, go jump into the pool.
Let's splishy, splash, splosh and have some fun,
Helping frog to jump off to get cool!

(13-Tune-Hey Diddle Diddle)

Wizzy's words

in go jump have help
frog off get

Catch the Ball, Baby

Catch the ball, baby, when it is hot,
If the cow moos, the bunny will hop.
If the cat meows, the duck will quack,
Catch the ball, baby, and throw it back.

(14-Tune-Hush-a-Bye Baby)

Wizzy’s words

catch ball baby hot cow bunny cat

meow(s) duck throw

Tickle, Tickle Monkey

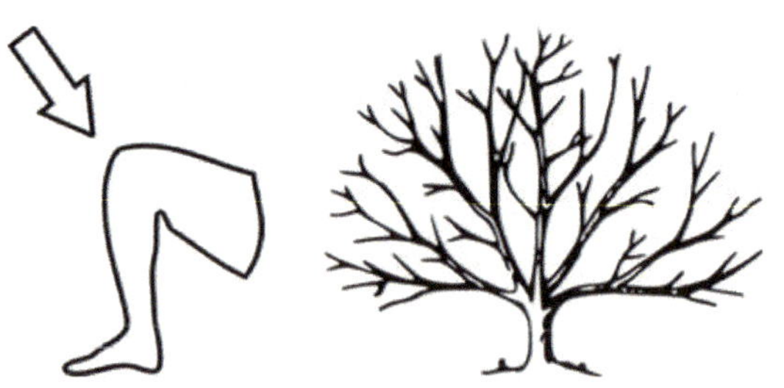

Tickle, tickle monkey under its big toe,
Now do the same but on the monkey's nose.
Then do the same at the back of its knee,
And tickle, tickle monkey, till it runs up the tree.

(15-Tune-Itsy Bitsy Spider)

Wizzy's words

tickle monkey under big toe on nose
knee run(s) up tree

Little Cold Bee

Little cold bee, wants to have tea,
But cannot see where to sit down.
In the porch with clean knife and fork,
Licking its lips with a frown.

(16-Tune-Little Bo Peep)

Wizzy's words

little cold bee want(s) have

tea see where sit down in clean

knife fork

Pretty, White Flower

Pretty, white flower, lands on my tummy,
Tickling my little tum!
You dance on me until I laugh with glee,
Before you fly off to the sun.

(17a-Tune-Little Jack Horner)

Wizzy's words

pretty white flower on

my tummy tickle little you

dance me off sun

Snowy, White Tiger

Snowy, white tiger sits in its hideout,
Keeping its ice-cream hot!
It sits in its chair and combs its long hair,
And then checks the slop in the pot!

(17b-Tune-Little Jack Horner)

Wizzy's words

snow(y) white tiger sit(s) in

ice-cream hot chair comb(s) hair

Mousy, Mousy, So Unwary

Mousy, Mousy, so unwary,
Why do you scamper out?
With little claws and dirty paws,
You've even got mud on your snout!

(18-Tune-Mary, Mary, Quite Contrary)

Wizzy's words

why? you out little dirty on

Knock-a-Knock

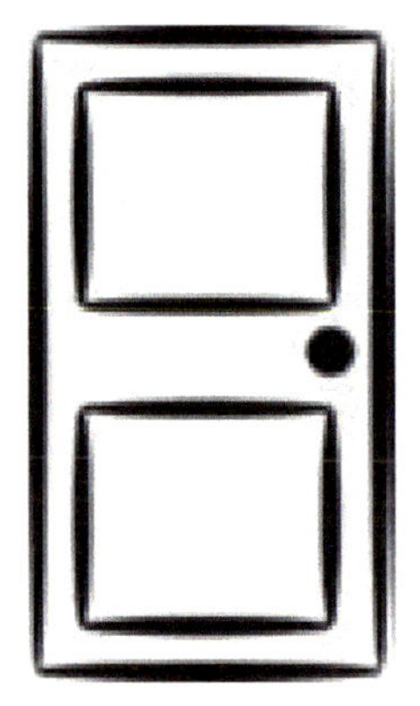

Knock-a-knock, knock-a-knock, little bug,
Come and sleep, hidden under the rug.
Push it and pull it, so it keeps you warm.
So, you're as snug as a bug and safe from the storm.

(19a-Tune-Pat-a-Cake)

Wizzy's words

knock little bug come
sleep under push

Knock-a-Knock

Knock-a-knock, knock-a-knock, postman stop!
Give me the gift and then off you pop.
Stroke it, love it. Oh! It's making me sneeze,
I do love this new puppy that's jumping on me!

(19b-Tune-Pat-a-Cake)

Wizzy’s words

knock stop give me off

you love make this puppy

that jump on

Wizzy Put Your Jacket On

Wizzy put your jacket on,
Wizzy put your jacket on,
Wizzy put your jacket on,
We want a walk!
Wizzy take it off again,
Wizzy take it off again,
Wizzy take it off again,
Rain's not gone away!

(20-Tune-Polly Put the Kettle On)

Wizzy's words

jacket on want walk take
off rain gone away

Foot, Finger...

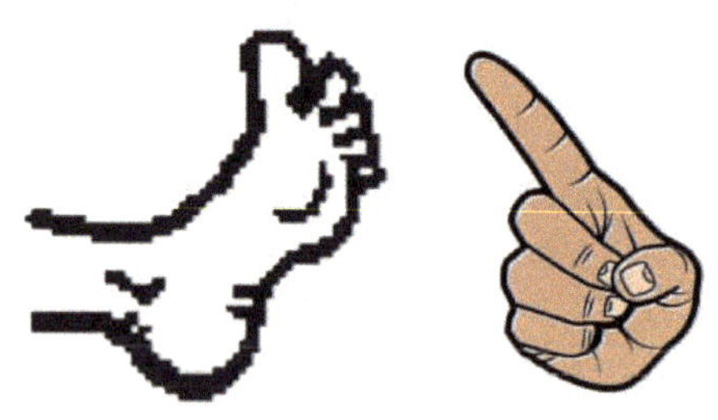

Foot, finger here, foot, finger there,
Foot, finger on my nose, near my hair.
Let's put it here, let's put it there,
Let's put it on my nose, near my hair.

(21-Tune-Pease Porridge)

Wizzy's words

foot finger here there

on my nose hair

'Thanks!' Say the Flowers!

Make a buzz like bumble bees do,
Buzz around the flowers.
This is how the flowers grow,
'Thanks!' say the flowers.
On and on the bumbling goes,
In and out the flowers.
This is how the flowers grow,
'Thanks!' say the flowers.

(22-Tune-Pop Goes the Weasel)

Wizzy's words

make bee(s) flower(s) this

thanks on goes in out

Ride a Red Bus to Elephant Zoo

Ride a red bus to elephant zoo,
Look at the tired baby, as it tries to move.
Standing close to mummy and close to its pool,
Splashing the water so it can keep cool.

(23-Tune-Ride a Cock Horse to Banbury Cross)

Wizzy's words

ride red bus elephant zoo look tired baby mummy water

Swing-a-Swing a Teddy

Swing-a-swing a teddy,
Let teddy's name be Freddy.
Together! Together!
Let's all sit down.

(24-Tune-Ring-a-Ring-o-Roses)

Wizzy's words

swing teddy all sit down

Read a Book Baby

Read a book baby, sat on my lap,
When your eyes close, the reading will stop.
When your lips close, the sleeping will start,
Then small, wee baby away I'll dart.

(25-Tune-Hush-a-Bye Baby)

Wizzy's words

read book baby on my eye(s) close

stop sleep away

Throw and Catch the Bubbles

Throw and catch the bubbles,
Dirty, yucky bear!
One bath,
Two baths!
Cleaning you everywhere!

(26-Tune-Round and Round the Garden...)

Wizzy's words

throw catch bubble(s) dirty yucky bear
one two bath(s) clean you

Explore, Dinosaurs' Roars

Explore, dinosaurs' roars,
See down the road through the windows.
Every day hear them stomp all the way,
And play along on the bongos!

(27-Tune-See-Saw, Margery Daw)

Wizzy's words

see down road window(s) on

Plane Fly, Plane High

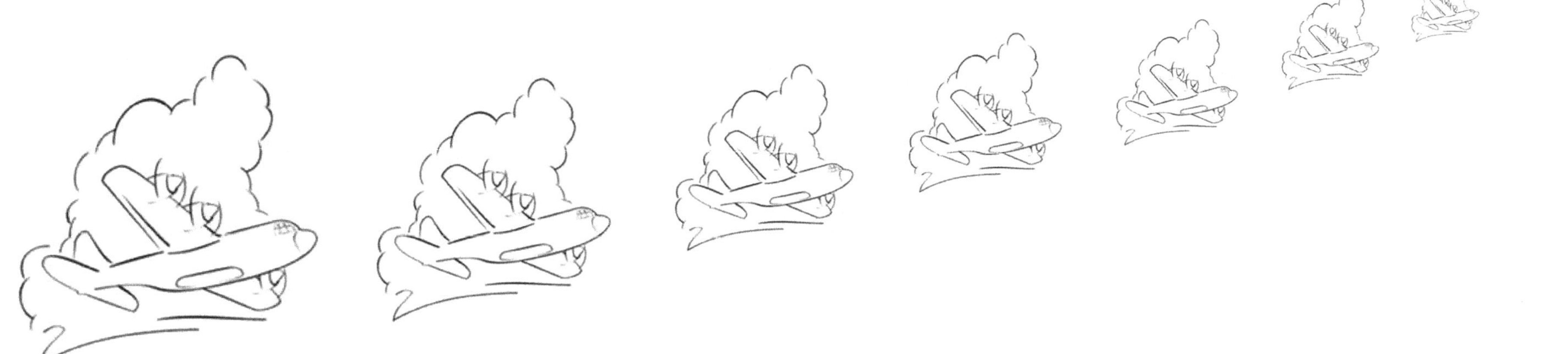

Plane fly, plane high,
I'll be on watch tonight.
Will it fly fast, all through the night?
It's already out of sight.

(28-Tune-Star Light, Star Bright)

Wizzy's words

plane on all night out

It’s Snowing and Cold

It’s snowing and cold and we have been told,
You must put your coats on going out, yes you!
You’ll play in the snow but keep yourselves warm,
And then come back in when you’re through, now shoo!

(29-Tune-The North Wind Doth Blow)

Wizzy's words

cold have you coat(s) on

out yes in snow come

The Frog So Green

The frog so green, could not be seen, up on the table top,
The bug so green, it was quite mean, and jumped and jumped non-stop.
The snake so green, said, 'You're so mean,' and told the bug to run,
The bug so green, stopped being so mean, and said, 'I'll be more fun.'

(30-Tune-The Queen of Hearts)

Wizzy's words

frog up on table bug

jump stop snake run more

There Was a Little Dog

There was a little dog, and it danced a little jig,
It stopped a little monkey, helping a little pig.
They stopped a little cat, that ate a little fish,
Then they all danced together in cat's little dish!

(31-Tune-There Was a Crooked Man)

Wizzy's words

there little dog dance stop

monkey help pig cat fish

This Hungry Monkey

This hungry monkey, ate its dinner,
This hungry monkey, had some bread,
This hungry monkey, ate some more,
This hungry monkey, was fed.
But still hungry monkey went...
Eat! Eat! Eat! I want more bread.

(32-Tune-This Little Piggy)

Wizzy's words

this hungry monkey dinner

bread more eat want

Two White Bikes

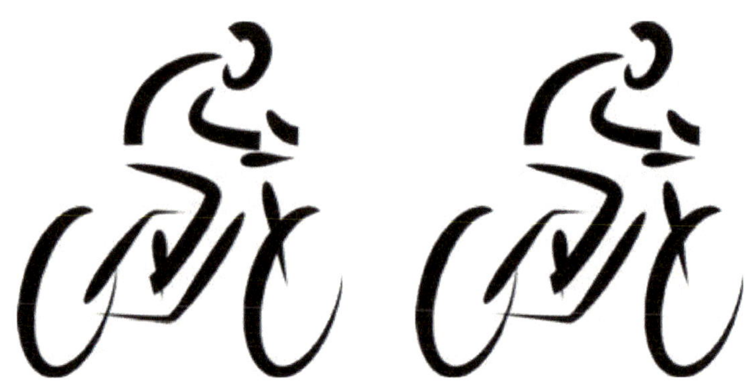

Two white bikes, two white bikes,
See how they go, see how they go,
They both go faster than Wizzy's kite,
They speed on their wheels, having such delight,
Will you ever have so much fun in your life,
As two white bikes?

(33-Tune-Three Blind Mice)

Wizzy's words

two white bike(s) see

go on you have in

Doctor, Doctor, I Feel Sick

Doctor, doctor, I feel sick,
Ate my dinner far too quick!
When you finish come to mine,
Think the burger was not fine!
Doctor, doctor, I feel sick,
Ate my dinner far too quick!

(34-Tune-Twinkle, Twinkle, Little Star)

Wizzy’s words

doctor my dinner you

come mine burger

Rubbish, Rubbish, in the Park

Rubbish, rubbish, in the park,
Fix and tidy before dark!
Bring paper from all places,
Work like robots with kind faces!
Rubbish, rubbish, in the park,
Fix and tidy before dark!

(35-Tune-Twinkle, Twinkle, Little Star)

Wizzy's words

rubbish in park fix dark

bring paper all faces

Slippers, Toothbrush, Sleepy Head

Slippers, toothbrush, sleepy head,
Time to jump up out of bed!
Good, it's breakfast, rumbling tum,
I do like crumpets, yum, yum!
Slippers, toothbrush, sleepy head,
Time to jump up out of bed!

(36-Tune-Twinkle, Twinkle, Little Star)

Wizzy's words

slipper(s) toothbrush sleep head jump

up out bed good breakfast

Coffee, Coffee, Bottle Too

Coffee, coffee, bottle too,
My hot coffee, milk for you.
Plate of grapes for you to eat,
Please sit safely for your treat.
Coffee, coffee, bottle too,
My hot coffee, milk for you.

(37-Tune-Twinkle, Twinkle, Little Star)

Wizzy's words

coffee bottle my hot milk plate

grape(s) you eat please sit

Balloon, Balloon, Pretty Thing

Balloon, balloon, pretty thing,
Keep on blowing in the wind.
Up above my head I clap,
Like a birdy in a flap.
Balloon, balloon, pretty thing,
Keep on blowing in the wind.

(38-Tune-Twinkle, Twinkle, Little Star)

Wizzy's words

balloon pretty on in up

my head clap bird

Cookie, Cookie, in My Mouth

Cookie, cookie, in my mouth,
Here is Wizzy in our house.
Wizzy helps to eat the food,
Oh dear! Baby wants some too!
Cookie, cookie, in my mouth,
Here is Wizzy in our house.

(39-Tune-Twinkle, Twinkle, Little Star)

Wizzy's words

cookie in my mouth here house

help(s) eat food baby wants

Pillow, Pillow, You're All Mine!

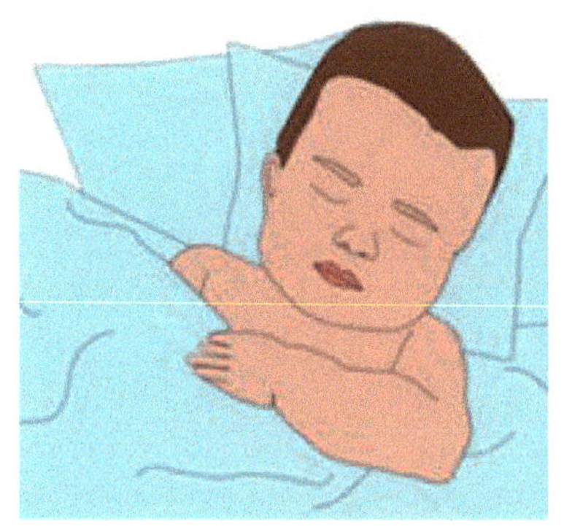

Pillow, pillow, you're all mine!
Keep me sleeping all the time.
By myself so fast asleep,
Happy dreaming with no peeps.
Pillow, pillow, you're all mine,
Keep me sleeping all the time.

(40-Tune-Twinkle, Twinkle, Little Star)

Wizzy's words

pillow all mine me

sleep myself happy

Welcome, Welcome, Garden Green

Welcome, welcome, garden green,
Bottom sat upon that swing.
Look and see, cute as can be,
A baby duck, looks at me.
Welcome, welcome, garden green,
Bottom sat upon that swing.

(41-Tune-Twinkle, Twinkle, Little Star)

Wizzy's words

welcome bottom that swing
look see baby duck me

My Paper, My Pencil...

My paper, my pencil,
My keys and my pen,
Are out of sight,
By the black hen!
Look by the window,
Then by the chair.
Open the curtains,
Then you'll find them there.

(42-Rhythm-see guide)

Wizzy’s words

my paper pencil key(s)

pen out black hen look

window chair open there

Days Lighter, Nights Darker...

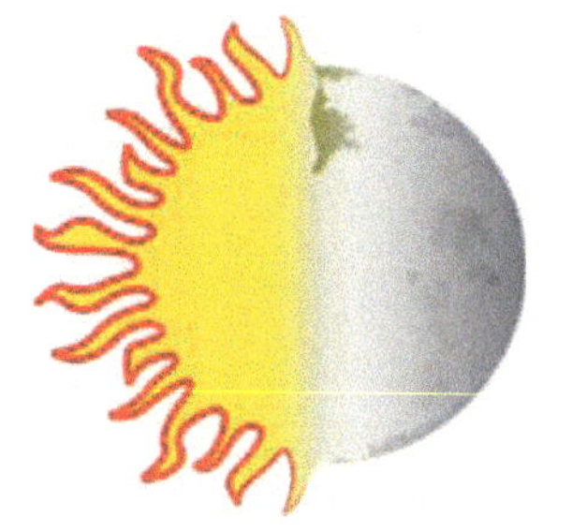

Days lighter, nights darker,
Sun shines, moon is bright.
Sun keeps us warm,
Then hides at night.
Watch the stars twinkling,
All through the night.
They'll be hiding too,
By the morning light.

(43-Rhythm-see guide)

Wizzy's words

dark sun moon night

star(s) all light

Car Talking to Garage...!

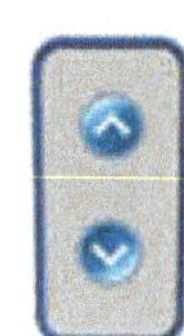

Car talking to garage!
'Don't leave me outside.'
Hit the button,
Let me inside.
You are being stinky,
I will get wet.
I don't need washing,
So please don't upset.

(44-Rhythm-see guide)

Wizzy’s words

car me outside hit you
stinky get wet wash please

Here Dancing to Radio...

Here dancing to radio,
The girl and the boy.
Look at their arms,
It's ships ahoy!
Look at their dance moves,
The speedy pair.
Wiggling and making,
High kicks in the air.

(45-Rhythm-see guide)

Wizzy's words

here radio girl boy look

arm(s) dance kick(s) in

Is Daddy the Gorilla...

Is daddy the gorilla,
At home for the day?
Or is he out,
With mum today?
Look in the cupboard,
Or in his lair.
Feeding or napping,
He goes everywhere!

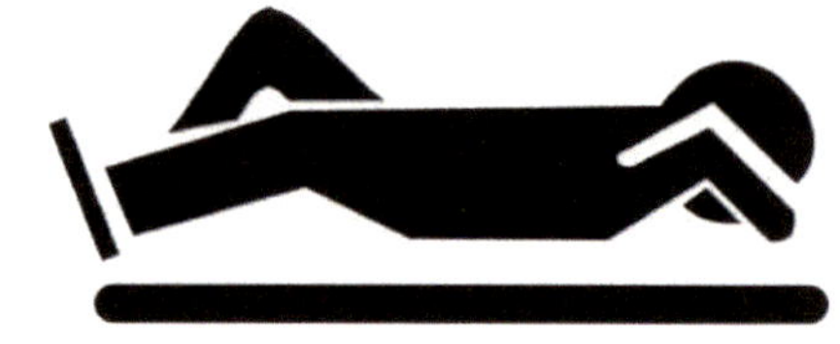

(46-Rhythm-see guide)

Wizzy's words

daddy/dad home out

mum/mummy look in

feed nap goes

Eat Apples and Oranges...

Eat apples and oranges,
And soup for your lunch.
Fill up the bowl,
Then go munch, munch.
Everyone's eating,
Without any haste.
Happy and healthy,
And proud there's no waste.

(47-Rhythm-see guide)

Wizzy's words

eat apple(s) orange(s) soup lunch up

bowl go happy

Oh! Turkey and Turtle...

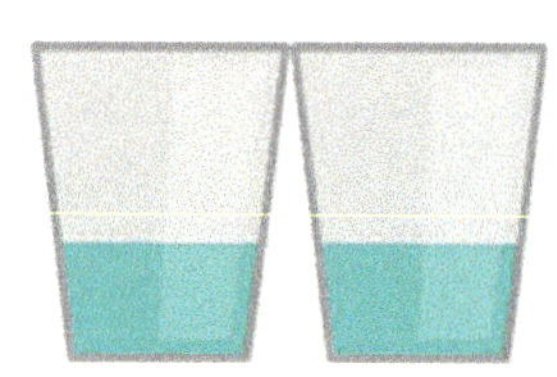

Oh, turkey and turtle!
Would you like a drink?
Each has a cough,
We need to think.
Bring a clean blanket,
And cover yourselves,
Snuggly and warmly,
Until you get well.

(48-Rhythm-see guide)

Wizzy's words

turkey turtle you drink cough

bring clean blanket get

No, Crackers and Burgers...

No, crackers and burgers,
Are not in this shop!
But juice is here,
So, in we'll pop.
Sit in the trolley,
Give me a kiss.
Elbow past biscuits,
They're not on our list.

(49-Rhythm-see guide)

Wizzy's words

no cracker(s) burger(s) in this shop juice here sit trolley give me kiss elbow biscuit(s) on

Put Butter and Ice-Cream...

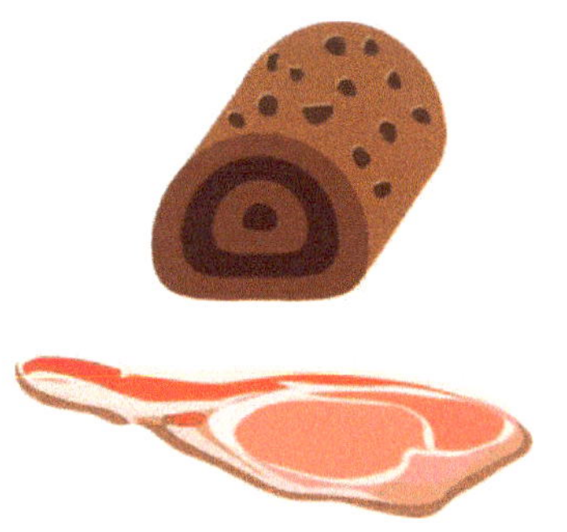

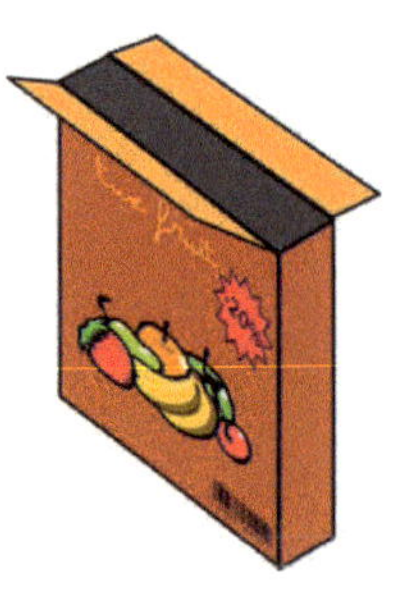

Put butter and ice-cream,
On the shopping list.
Add cake and meat,
You get the gist?
Then add cereal,
And a truck of jelly!
No, not bananas,
No room in my belly!

(50-Rhythm-see guide)

Wizzy's words

butter ice-cream on shop cake

meat you get cereal truck

no banana(s) in belly

A Tissue, A Tissue...

A tissue, a tissue,
I need when I sneeze.
Cat goes meow,
I go to wheeze.
It's just struck seven,
See on the clock?
Tishoo-a-tishoo,
I wish I could stop!

(51-Rhythm-see guide)

Wizzy's words

tissue cat goes meow go

seven see on clock stop

My Belly Is Empty...

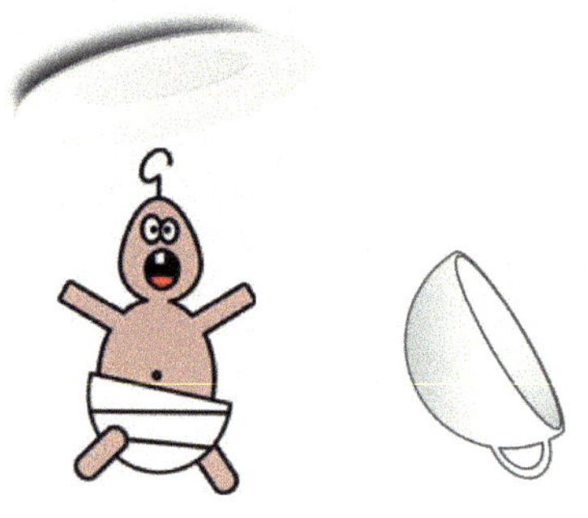

My belly is empty,
It needs to be fed.
Cup on the floor,
Bowl on my head!
Let's change my nappy,
Then get some toast.
Chewing and teething,
I love toast the most.

(52-Rhythm-see guide)

Wizzy's words

my belly cup on floor bowl

head nappy get toast love

We’re Wearing Glasses...

We’re wearing glasses,
To see the wee boat.
Horse in the field,
In its overcoat.
Look at its baby,
With wobbly legs.
Stumbling and kneeling,
Legs looking like pegs.

(53-Rhythm-see guide)

Wizzy's words

glasses see wee boat horse

in look baby leg(s) knee

I've Broken the Mirror...

I've broken the mirror,
Fell in the potty!
I've no money,
Gran's gone dotty.
Let's find some paper,
Use soap as glue!
Sticking and pasting,
Mirror looks like new!

(54-Rhythm-see guide)

Wizzy's words

broken mirror in potty no

money gran paper soap

Off, Hooting to Station...

Off, hooting to station,
Goes Bizzy the train.
Stop at the school,
Push off again.
To the hospital,
Then to the church.
Kneeling and praying,
For peace, people search.

(55-Rhythm-see guide)

Wizzy's words

off goes train stop school

push hospital church

Put Crayons and All Dolls...

Put crayons and all dolls,
Right under the stairs.
Use both your hands,
Put shoes in pairs!
Under the sofa,
Look for the spoon!
Plate's on the table,
And dinner is soon.

(56-Rhythm-see guide)

Wizzy's words

crayon(s) all doll(s) under stairs

hand(s) shoe(s) in sofa look

spoon plate on table dinner

It’s Crispy and Crunchy...

It’s crispy and crunchy,
And sticks to your chin.
Hold with your thumb,
Sink your teeth in.
It’s full of garlic,
Bath before bed!
Smelly but tasty,
Is my garlic bread.

(57-Rhythm-see guide)

Wizzy's words

crisp chin thumb teeth in

bath bed my bread

Whilst Eating My Dinner...

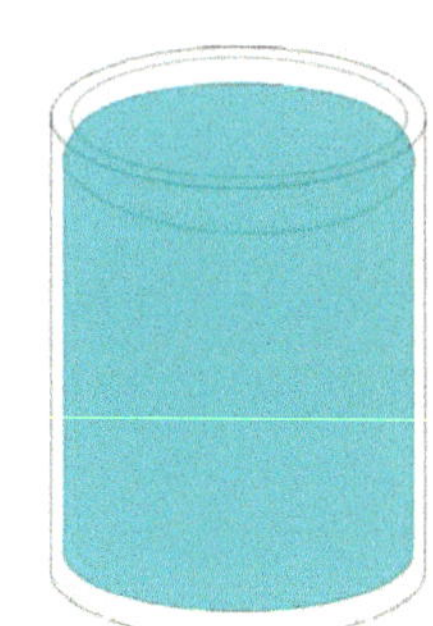

Whilst eating my dinner,
In my yellow hat.
I wear my watch,
And feed the cat.
Eating spaghetti,
Is so much fun.
Glass full of water,
For when I am done.

(58-Rhythm-see guide)

Wizzy's words

eat my dinner in yellow hat watch

feed cat spaghetti glass water

I'm Running and Skipping...

I'm running and skipping,
In my shirt and socks.
Put more clothes on!
Blocks in the box!
No, you're not playing,
With no pants on!
Dressing up quickly,
Will not take too long.

(59-Rhythm-see guide)

Wizzy's words

run in my shirt sock(s) more on

block(s) no pants dress up take

We're Washing and Dressing...

We're washing and dressing,
Then boots and gloves on.
Look at the birds,
Singing their song.
Ears are for hearing,
The soft birdsong.
Cheeping and chirping,
We all sing along.

(60-Rhythm-see guide)

Wizzy's words

wash dress boots glove(s) on

look bird(s) ear(s) all sing

My Bright, Shiny Penny...

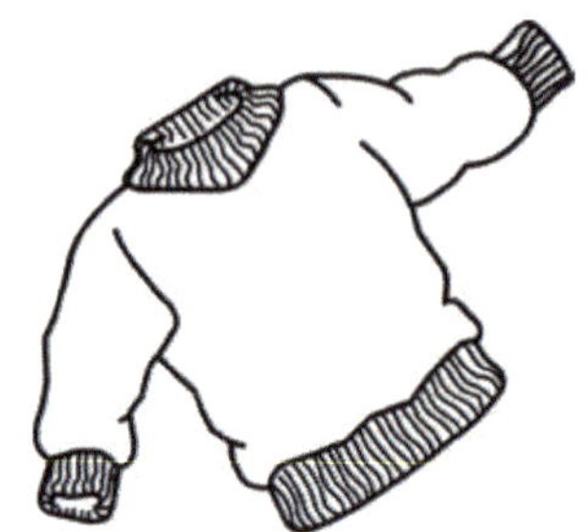

My bright, shiny penny,
In my pocket lies.
I brush it clean,
Hide it from spies.
Put on my jumper,
It's out of sight.
Hidden so safely,
Out of the daylight.

(61-Rhythm-see guide)

Wizzy's words

my penny in pocket brush

clean on jumper out

You’re Ready and Steady...

You’re ready and steady,
To go on a ride.
Strap round your neck,
Let’s motorbike!
Fast as my pushchair,
Excuse me do!
Faster and faster,
Be back after noon.

(62-Rhythm-see guide)

Wizzy's words

go on ride neck motorbike my

pushchair excuse me (scuse me)

On Trainers, Off Trainers...

On trainers, off trainers,
Let's go back to sleep.
Go back to bed,
Alarm will beep.
Stay in pyjamas,
Back in the cot.
Baby's not waking,
Till seven o'clock.

(63-Rhythm-see guide)

Wizzy's words

on trainer(s) off go sleep bed
in pyjamas cot baby seven

It's Seven, It's Seven...

It's seven, it's seven,
Awake from your cot.
Fetch a towel,
Right on the dot.
Fill sink with water,
Splash all over.
Dressing clean baby,
In new pullover.

(64-Rhythm-see guide)

Wizzy's words

seven cot towel on sink

water all dress clean baby in

From City to City...

From city to city,
You'll find lots of books.
Go on inside,
You will be hooked.
In the library,
Lots you can see.
Stories and info,
For everybody.

(65-Rhythm-see guide)

Wizzy's words

book(s) go on you

in library see

Oh! Numbers, Oh! Numbers...

Oh! Numbers, Oh! Numbers,
You are so much fun.
Count up to ten,
Starting at one.
Then, move on to two,
Then, count to three.
Slowly then quickly,
Keep counting with me.

(66-Rhythm-see guide)

Wizzy's words

you up ten one on
two three me

Oh! Numbers, Oh! Numbers...

Oh! Numbers, Oh! Numbers,
You make me count you.
On your fingers,
Show me a two.
Then, go up to three,
Do take your time.
Counting and counting,
From one up to nine.

(67-Rhythm-see guide)

Wizzy's words

you make me on finger(s) show two

go up three take one nine

Oh! Numbers, Oh! Numbers...

Oh! Numbers, Oh! Numbers,
You're stuck on my door.
I see a five,
And see a four.
Count along with me,
Don't miss the six.
Counting and counting,
Which one would you pick?

(68-Rhythm-see guide)

Wizzy's words

on my door see five four

me six one you

Oh! Numbers, Oh! Numbers...

Oh! Numbers, Oh! Numbers,
I can see an eight.
Count on fingers,
Or on the gates.
Do count it with me,
Look, it's a ten.
Singing and dancing,
Ten big fluffy hens.

(69-Rhythm-see guide)

Wizzy's words

see eight on finger(s) me

look ten sing dance big hen(s)

Happy Birthday to You, Not Me!

Happy birthday to you, yes, yes, yes.
Happy birthday to me, no, no, no.
Happy birthday dear you-oo,
Happy birthday to you.

(70-Tune-Happy Birthday to You)

Wizzy’s words

you yes me no

Full List of Wizzy's Words

A	balloon	bird(s)	bottle	bubble(s)	car
all	banana(s)	biscuit(s)	bottom	bug	cat
apple(s)	bath(s)	black	bowl	bunny	catch
arm(s)	bear	blanket	boy	burger(s)	cereal
away	bed	block(s)	bread	bus	chair
B	bee(s)	blue	breakfast	butter	cheese
baby	belly	boat	bring	bye-bye	chicken
bad	big	book(s)	broken	**C**	chin
ball	bike(s)	boot(s)	brush	cake	church

clap	cookie	**D**	door	eight	fish
clean	cot	daddy	down	elbow	five
clock	cough	dance	dress	elephant	fix
close	cow	dark	drink	excuse me (scuse me)	floor
coat(s)	cracker(s)	dinner	duck	eye(s)	flower
coffee	crayon(s)	dirty	**E**	**F**	food
cold	crisp	doctor	ear(s)	face(s)	foot
comb	cup	dog	eat	feed	fork
come	cut	doll(s)	egg(s)	finger	four

frog	goes	hat	home	in	kiss
G	gone	have	horse	**J**	knee
get	good	head	hospital	jacket	knife
girl	gran	heavy	hot	juice	knock
give	grape(s)	hello	house	jump	**L**
glass	**H**	help	hug	jumper	leg(s)
glasses	hair	hen(s)	hungry	**K**	library
glove(s)	hand(s)	here	**I**	key(s)	light
go	happy	hit	ice-cream	kick(s)	little

look	mine	my	nose	**P**	pizza(s)
love	mirror	myself	**O**	pants	plane
lunch	money	**N**	off	paper	plate
M	monkey	nap	on	park	please
make	moon	nappy	one	pen	pocket
me	more	neck	open	pencil	potty
meat	motorbike	night	orange(s)	penny	pretty
meow	mouth	nine	out	pig	puppy
milk	mummy	no		pillow	push

pushchair	road	shirt	slide	spoon	take
pyjamas	room	shoe(s)	slipper(s)	stairs	tea
R	rubbish	shop	snake	star(s)	teddy
radio	run	show	snow	stinky	teeth
rain	**S**	sing	soap	stop	ten
ran	school	sink	sock(s)	sun	thanks
read	see	sit	sofa	swing	that
red	seven	six	soup	**T**	there
ride	sheep	sleep	spaghetti	table	this

three	toothbrush	turtle	watch	**Y**
throw	towel	two	water	yellow
thumb	train	**U**	wee	yes
tickle	trainers	under	welcome	you
tiger	tree	up	wet	your
tired	trolley	**W**	where	yucky
tissue	truck	walk	white	**Z**
toast	tummy	want	why	zoo
toe	turkey	wash	window(s)